Restoration - Setting The Bone

Joshua Rhoades

Published by Joshua Paul Rhoades, 2024.

While every precaution has been taken in the preparation of this book, the publisher assumes no responsibility for errors or omissions, or for damages resulting from the use of the information contained herein.

RESTORATION - SETTING THE BONE

First edition. August 31, 2024.

ISBN: 979-8227506580

Written by Joshua Rhoades.

of duty not only to my family but also to the cause they were fighting for. This sense of duty brought me before King Saul, who, upon hearing my bold offer to fight Goliath, expressed severe doubts about my abilities. He looked upon my youthful frame and could not see how I, with no armor or sword, could face such a fearsome giant.Goliath himself, towering and menacing, mocked me as I stepped onto the battlefield, his words heavy with contempt and surety of victory. His towering figure clad in armor, with a spear like a weaver's beam, seemed invincible. Yet, as he taunted me, I felt a profound calm settle over me; I knew that the battle was not mine but the Lord's. I declared as much to Goliath, telling him that the God of the armies of Israel whom he had defied would deliver him into my hands. With a simple sling and a stone, and faith as my greatest weapon, I struck the Philistine on his forehead. The giant fell face down to the ground, and I stood over him, a boy no longer underestimated but recognized as the instrument through which God showed His power.This historical moment is not merely a testament to my personal courage but serves as a beacon of inspiration for every Christian facing their own "Goliaths." Whether these giants are doubts, fears, or seemingly insurmountable challenges, the story exemplifies how faith in God equips us to overcome them. The practical lessons derived from this experience emphasize the importance of obedience, humility, and trust in God's power over our own. In moments of trial, we, like I once did, can draw strength from understanding that God's purposes will prevail over our adversities. As I recount my stand on the battlefield, it becomes clear that true victory in life comes from putting our faith into action, trusting in the Lord's guidance, and stepping forward with courage, even when the odds seem overwhelmingly against us.

Also by Joshua Rhoades

Courage Under Fire: David's Stand On The Battlefield

Jonah's Journey: Voices Of Redemption And Lessons In Obedience

The Furnace Of Faith: 12 Principles From The Heat Of Faith

Whispers of Hope: Inspiring Stories of Men's Prayers In Scripture

Frontier Legends: The Oregon Dream

Elijah: A Beacon Of Boldness

HOOK, LINE & SAVIOUR - Faith Reflections from Fishing

Driven By Faith: Motor Racing Inspired Christian Life

30 Day Devotional - Bold and Strong- Coffee Devotions for a Courageous Christian Walk

Authentic Christianity: The Heart of Old Time Religion

Consider The Ant - God's Tiny Preachers

Flee Fornication: The Plea For Purity

Renewed Hope- How to Find Encouragement in God

Sounding The Call - The Voice of Conviction

The Altar - Where Heaven Meets Earth

The Bible's Battlefields- Timeless Lessons from Ancient Wars

The Sacred Art of Silence - How Silence Speaks in Scripture

Under Fire- The Sanctity of the Traditional Biblical Home

Who Is on the Lord's Side? A Call to Righteousness

What Is Truth? - From Skepticism to Submission

First and Goal- Faith and Football Fundamentals
From Dugout to Devotion- Spiritual Lessons from Baseball
Par for the Course- Faith and Fairways
The Believer's Pace- Tools for Running Life's Marathon
The Immutable Fortress- Security in God's Unchanging Nature
Biblical Bravery
Jesus Knows- Our Hearts, Our Responsibility
Restoration - Setting The Bone
The Jezebel Effect - Ancient Manipulations Modern Lessons
The Shout That Stopped The Saviour

Introduction

"Restoration: Setting the Bone" dives into the profound biblical concept of restoration, exploring the journey of a Christian seeking to be made whole again after experiencing spiritual, emotional, or moral brokenness. Just as a physician sets a fractured bone to promote healing and ensure proper function, God's process of restoration involves careful, deliberate actions that realign us with His will, mend our brokenness, and restore us to full spiritual health.

The imagery of setting a bone is powerful and apt for describing the restoration process. A broken bone left unattended can heal improperly, leading to ongoing pain and dysfunction. Similarly, when Christians experience spiritual fractures—whether due to sin, trauma, or life's trials—ignoring the need for restoration can result in ongoing spiritual pain and an impaired ability to live out God's purpose. This book is a guide for those who recognize their need for healing and are seeking God's methodical and loving touch to restore them to wholeness.

The Bible is rich with examples of God's restorative work. From the fall of Adam and Eve and the subsequent promise of redemption to the many stories of individuals like King David, who, after falling into deep sin, experienced God's restorative grace, Scripture teaches us that no matter how broken we are, God is willing and able to restore us. In Psalm 51:10, David cries out, "Create in me a clean heart, O God; and renew a right spirit within me." This plea captures the essence of what it means to seek restoration—to recognize our brokenness and humbly ask God to do the deep work of healing and renewing our hearts.

Restoration is not always a quick or easy process. Just as setting a bone can be painful and requires time to heal, spiritual restoration often involves difficult, yet necessary, steps. It may require confession, repentance, forgiveness, and a willingness to let go of the past and trust God with the future. But just as a properly set bone regains strength and functionality, a soul that undergoes God's restorative process emerges stronger, more resilient, and better equipped to fulfill God's purpose.

"Restoration: Setting the Bone" will walk you through the biblical principles of restoration, offering insights into how God works to heal our deepest wounds and how we can cooperate with Him in this process. Whether you are seeking restoration for yourself or walking alongside someone else in their journey, this book will provide the tools and encouragement needed to embrace God's healing power.

We will explore the steps involved in restoration, such as acknowledging our need for healing, surrendering to God's will, embracing the discomfort of the process, and trusting in God's ultimate plan for our lives. Throughout, we will be reminded of the hope that is found in God's promises—that no matter how fractured our lives may seem, God is a master at setting the bone and bringing us back to a place of strength, purpose, and peace.

In "Restoration: Setting the Bone," you will find not only the hope of healing but also the assurance that God is with you every step of the way, gently and lovingly guiding you toward complete restoration.

Chapter 1 - Perception of the Problem

Understanding the problem is the first and most important step in both physical healing and spiritual restoration. In the case of a physical injury, like a broken bone, identifying exactly where and how the bone is fractured is crucial. A doctor must carefully examine the injury, often using tools like X-rays, to see inside the body and understand what has happened. This process of diagnosis is called "perception of the problem." The doctor must be very accurate because the next steps depend entirely on understanding the exact nature of the fracture. If the doctor doesn't identify the problem correctly, the treatment may not work, and the bone could heal improperly, leading to more pain or even permanent damage. Similarly, in Christian restoration, perception of the problem is equally important. The Bible, in Galatians 6:1, teaches that when someone is caught in a fault or sin, those who are spiritual should help to restore that person. However, this must be done in a spirit of meekness, meaning with humility and gentleness. Just as a doctor needs to carefully examine a broken bone to understand how to treat it, Christians need to carefully perceive the spiritual problem in someone's life to help restore them properly. This verse also reminds believers to be cautious, considering their own weaknesses, so they are not tempted to fall into the same sin. Recognizing a spiritual issue is like seeing the fracture in a bone. It requires spiritual insight and wisdom. If the problem is ignored or not fully understood, any attempts at restoration might not be effective. For example, if someone is struggling with anger, it might be easy to see the outbursts without understanding the deeper issue that is causing that anger. Maybe the person is dealing with unresolved hurt or fear. Just like a doctor looks beyond the surface to see the full extent of a fracture, Christians need to look beyond the obvious symptoms of sin to understand the root causes. This perception allows for a more careful and gentle approach to restoration, which is essential for healing. Just as setting a bone correctly is critical for physical healing, addressing the real issue in someone's spiritual life is critical for their restoration. A gentle approach is necessary because, just like a broken bone, a person's spirit can be fragile when they are dealing with sin or failure. Harsh words or actions could do more harm than good, just like rough handling of a broken bone could make the injury worse. Instead, a gentle and careful approach can help to bring healing and restoration, both physically and spiritually. In summary, perception of the problem, whether it is a broken bone or a spiritual issue, is the first and most crucial step toward healing. It requires careful examination and a gentle approach to ensure that the treatment or restoration is effective and leads to true healing. Whether in the medical field or in spiritual life, recognizing the problem correctly sets the foundation for everything that follows. This careful perception ensures that the process of healing, whether setting a bone or restoring someone spiritually, is done with the wisdom and care needed to bring about complete and lasting recovery.

Chapter 2 - Positioning (Re-aligning the Bone)

Positioning, especially in the context of bone setting, is a critical step that follows the perception of the problem. Once a doctor has identified that a bone is broken, the next crucial step is to reposition the bone correctly. This process is called "reduction" in medical terms, but it can also be simply understood as re-aligning the bone. Imagine if you had a broken arm or leg, and the bones inside were out of place. If the bones are not correctly aligned, they can't heal properly. The body is designed to heal itself, but it needs the bones to be in the right position for the healing process to work. If the bones are not positioned correctly, they might heal crooked, which could cause more pain and limit how you can use that arm or leg in the future. It might even require surgery to fix it later on. So, positioning the bone is about making sure that it is in the correct place, so that when the body begins to heal, everything comes back together as it should. This process can be painful and often requires the doctor to move the bone manually, sometimes using special tools or even surgery in more severe cases. The doctor has to be very precise because even a small misalignment can cause long-term problems. In a spiritual context, positioning is just as important. In Psalm 51:10, the Bible talks about creating a clean heart and renewing a right spirit. This is a prayer asking God to help reposition the heart and spirit of a person. Just as a broken bone needs to be re-aligned to heal properly, a person's heart and spirit need to be aligned with God's will for spiritual healing and growth. When someone has drifted away from what is right, their heart can become hardened or their spirit can become troubled. This is like a bone that has been dislocated or broken. It's not in the right place, and as a result, the person's life may be out of balance. They might feel lost, confused, or in pain, just like someone with a broken bone. The process of spiritual positioning involves asking God to help put things back in their proper place. This can be a painful process, just like physical bone setting, because it might involve confronting things that are difficult to face, such as past mistakes, sins, or bad habits. But just as the doctor knows how to reposition a bone, God knows how to realign a person's heart and spirit. This realignment is essential for spiritual healing and growth. Without it, a person's life might continue to be out of balance, leading to further pain or difficulties down the road. In both physical and spiritual contexts, proper positioning is key to healing. Without it, the body or the spirit cannot function as intended. When a bone is correctly aligned, the body can begin to heal, knitting the bone back together. When a heart and spirit are aligned with God's will, the person can begin to experience peace, joy, and a renewed sense of purpose. It's about making sure that everything is in the right place so that healing can occur naturally and fully. In the same way that a doctor carefully positions a bone to ensure proper healing, God carefully guides and helps position a person's heart and spirit to ensure their spiritual well-being. This process of positioning, whether it is physical or spiritual, is not just about fixing what is broken, but about restoring the person to their full potential. When the bone is positioned correctly, the person can eventually regain full use of the limb. When the heart and spirit are positioned correctly, the person can fully live out their faith and purpose. This process requires trust in the one doing the positioning—whether it is a doctor with a bone or God with a heart. Just as you would trust a doctor to set your broken bone, trusting God to reposition your heart and spirit is crucial for healing. In summary, positioning, or re-aligning, is an essential step in both physical and spiritual healing. It's about making sure everything is in the right place so that healing can occur properly. In bone setting, this means physically moving the bone back to where it should be. In Christian restoration, it means asking God to create a clean heart and renew a right spirit, aligning a person's inner life with God's will. Both processes require precision, care, and sometimes involve discomfort, but they are necessary steps toward complete healing and restoration. Proper positioning ensures that what is broken can be made whole again, allowing the person to move forward in life with strength and purpose. Just as a bone that is correctly aligned will heal properly and restore full function, a heart and spirit that are aligned with God will lead to a fulfilling and meaningful life.

Chapter 3 - Protection (Casting or Splinting)

Protection is a vital part of both physical healing and spiritual restoration, and it plays a crucial role in ensuring that the process of recovery goes smoothly and effectively. When someone breaks a bone, one of the first things a doctor does after setting the bone in the correct position is to apply a cast or a splint. This is a protective measure to keep the bone in place, allowing it to heal without any further injury or disruption. The cast or splint acts like a shield, surrounding the injured area and preventing any movement that could cause the bone to shift or become misaligned again. It is important because, without this protection, the bone might move out of place, which could lead to improper healing, prolonged pain, or even the need for surgery. The cast or splint also helps to keep the bone stable, reducing the pain and providing the necessary environment for the body to naturally heal the fracture. This protective measure must be kept on for a certain period, which might be weeks or even months, depending on the severity of the break. During this time, the person must be careful not to put too much pressure on the injured area, follow the doctor's instructions, and avoid activities that could cause more harm. Similarly, in the process of Christian restoration, protection is equally important. Psalm 46:10 says, "Be still, and know that I am God: I will be exalted among the heathen, I will be exalted in the earth." This verse speaks to the importance of being still and resting in God's presence as a form of protection. Just as a broken bone needs a cast or splint to keep it safe and secure, a person going through spiritual restoration needs to find stillness and peace in God's presence. This is a time to stop striving, worrying, or trying to fix everything on their own, and instead, trust that God is in control and that He is working on their behalf. Being still in God's presence means allowing Him to protect and guide the healing process without interference. It means trusting that He knows what is best, even when things seem uncertain or difficult. This kind of spiritual protection is crucial because, during times of restoration, a person can feel vulnerable, just like a broken bone that is fragile and in need of extra care. Without this protection, it's easy to fall back into old habits, negative thinking, or the very issues that caused the need for restoration in the first place. In the same way that a cast or splint prevents a bone from moving and getting injured again, being still in God's presence helps protect a person's heart and mind from the distractions and dangers of the world that could disrupt their spiritual healing. This period of protection might also involve setting boundaries, avoiding certain situations, or spending more time in prayer and reflection to stay connected to God. Just as a person with a broken bone must avoid certain activities and be cautious to protect their injury, a person undergoing spiritual restoration must also be mindful of their spiritual environment, ensuring they are in a safe and supportive space where they can heal without being pulled back into negative patterns. Protection during this time is not just about being physically still; it is also about creating a mental and spiritual environment that fosters healing. This could mean focusing on positive thoughts, surrounding oneself with supportive people, or engaging in activities that strengthen faith and encourage spiritual growth. It's about ensuring that nothing interferes with the healing process, just like how a cast or splint ensures the bone heals properly by keeping it immobilized. Moreover, just as a doctor monitors the healing of a bone to ensure the cast or splint is doing its job, a person in spiritual restoration should also check in with God regularly, through prayer, reading the Bible, or seeking counsel from trusted spiritual mentors, to ensure they are staying on the right path. This ongoing protection helps to prevent setbacks and keeps the person moving forward in their healing journey. The length of time this protection is needed can vary. For a bone, it depends on how severe the break was and how well the person follows the doctor's advice. For spiritual restoration, the time spent in stillness and protection in God's presence can also vary, depending on the person's unique situation and how deeply they need to heal. However, just like with a broken bone, rushing the process or neglecting the need for protection can lead to incomplete healing or even further damage. It is important to remain patient and allow the necessary time for complete restoration. In both cases, the ultimate goal of protection is to ensure that the healing is thorough and that, once the process is complete, the person can return to normal life—whether that means using the healed limb or living a spiritually restored life—without fear of re-injury or relapse. The protection provided by a cast or splint for a bone, and by God's presence for the spirit, is a temporary but essential phase of healing that must not be overlooked. It is a time of careful attention, gentle care, and trust in the process. In conclusion, protection, whether it involves casting or splinting for a broken bone, or finding stillness in God's presence for spiritual restoration, is a crucial part of the healing journey. It ensures that what is broken is kept safe from further harm, providing the necessary environment for healing to occur naturally and fully. By allowing this protective phase to do its work, a person can heal properly, without complications, and be restored to full strength, whether physically or spiritually. Just as a cast or splint eventually comes off when the bone is fully healed, the need for intense spiritual protection will also lessen as the person becomes stronger and more grounded in their faith. However, the importance of this protective phase cannot be overstated, as it lays the foundation for complete and lasting recovery, ensuring that both the body and the spirit are made whole again, ready to face the world with renewed strength and confidence.

Chapter 4 - Pain Management

Pain management is a crucial aspect of both physical healing and spiritual restoration, and it plays a significant role in ensuring that the recovery process is as smooth and effective as possible. When someone experiences a broken bone, one of the first and most important concerns is managing the pain that comes with it. Pain is the body's natural response to injury, and it serves as a signal that something is wrong and needs attention. However, while pain is a useful indicator, it can also be overwhelming and debilitating if not properly managed. In the case of a broken bone, the pain can be intense, especially right after the injury occurs. This is why doctors often focus on alleviating pain as part of the initial treatment. They might use medications like painkillers or even anesthesia if the pain is severe and needs to be controlled immediately. This helps the patient feel more comfortable and allows the doctors to perform necessary procedures, such as setting the bone or applying a cast, without causing additional distress. Pain management in this context is not just about making the patient feel better in the moment; it is also about enabling the healing process to begin. When the pain is under control, the body can focus on healing the injury rather than being in a constant state of stress and discomfort. Additionally, effective pain management can prevent the pain from becoming chronic, which can happen if the initial pain is not adequately addressed. Chronic pain can lead to long-term physical and emotional issues, making recovery much more difficult. Therefore, managing pain early and effectively is key to ensuring a smooth and successful recovery from a physical injury like a broken bone. In a similar way, pain management is also essential in the process of Christian restoration. Spiritual pain can come from a variety of sources, such as guilt, shame, loss, or the consequences of sin. This kind of pain, much like physical pain, signals that something is wrong and needs to be addressed. However, just as with physical pain, spiritual pain can be overwhelming and can hinder the healing process if it is not properly managed. In 2 Corinthians 12:9, the Bible says, "And he said unto me, My grace is sufficient for thee: for my strength is made perfect in weakness." This verse highlights the importance of God's grace in managing spiritual pain. God's grace acts as a form of pain management, providing comfort, strength, and peace to those who are hurting. Just as a doctor might provide pain relief to a patient with a broken bone, God offers His grace to help alleviate the spiritual pain that can accompany times of difficulty, failure, or loss. This grace is not just about making the pain go away; it is about enabling the healing process to take place. When someone is spiritually hurting, they might feel weak, vulnerable, and overwhelmed, but God's grace is there to support them, giving them the strength they need to face their pain and begin to heal. This spiritual pain management is essential because, without it, the pain can become too much to bear, leading to despair, bitterness, or a sense of hopelessness. Just as unmanaged physical pain can turn into chronic pain, unmanaged spiritual pain can lead to long-term spiritual damage, making it harder for the person to recover and move forward. However, with God's grace, the pain can be managed, allowing the person to focus on healing and growing in their faith. This grace does not necessarily remove the pain entirely, but it makes it bearable and provides the strength needed to endure it. In both physical and spiritual contexts, pain management is about more than just relief; it is about creating the right conditions for healing. In the case of a broken bone, effective pain management allows the body to relax and begin the process of mending the fracture. In the case of spiritual restoration, God's grace allows the person to find peace and strength in the midst of their pain, enabling them to work through their struggles and come out stronger on the other side. Pain management also involves recognizing that pain, while uncomfortable, is a natural part of the healing process. Just as a broken bone hurts because the body is signaling that something is wrong, spiritual pain can be a sign that something in a person's life needs to change or be addressed. This pain can lead to growth and deeper understanding if managed properly. By addressing the pain, whether through medication and care for a physical injury or through prayer, reflection, and reliance on God's grace for a spiritual injury, the healing process can proceed in a healthy and effective way. It is important to remember that pain, in both cases, is temporary and that managing it well is key to ensuring a full and lasting recovery. In summary, pain management is an essential part of both physical healing and spiritual restoration. For a broken bone, this involves using medications and other treatments to alleviate pain so that the body can focus on healing the injury. For spiritual restoration, pain management comes in the form of God's grace, which provides comfort, strength, and peace to help manage the spiritual pain that can accompany times of difficulty and growth. In both cases, managing the pain is crucial to ensuring that the healing process can take place effectively and that the person can recover fully, whether from a physical injury or from a spiritual struggle. By recognizing the importance of pain management and addressing it properly, the path to recovery becomes much smoother, allowing for complete healing and the ability to move forward with strength and confidence.

Chapter 5 - Periodic Check-ups

Periodic check-ups are a critical aspect of both physical healing and spiritual restoration, playing an essential role in ensuring that the recovery process is on the right track and that everything is progressing as it should. When someone suffers from a broken bone, the initial treatment, which might involve setting the bone and applying a cast or splint, is only the beginning of the healing journey. After this initial phase, it is crucial for the patient to have regular check-ups with their doctor to monitor the healing process. These check-ups are important because they allow the doctor to assess how well the bone is mending, whether it is staying in the correct position, and if there are any complications that need to be addressed. For instance, the doctor might take follow-up X-rays to ensure that the bone is properly aligned and that the body is effectively knitting the bone back together. Without these periodic check-ups, there's a risk that the bone might heal improperly, leading to long-term problems such as deformity, reduced mobility, or even chronic pain. In some cases, if the bone is not healing as expected, the doctor might need to adjust the treatment plan, perhaps by repositioning the bone, changing the cast, or recommending additional therapies like physical therapy. These check-ups also provide an opportunity for the patient to ask questions, express any concerns they might have about their healing process, and receive guidance on how to take care of the injury to promote the best possible recovery. Just as in the physical healing of a broken bone, periodic check-ups are equally important in the process of Christian restoration. In Philippians

1:6, the Bible says, "Being confident of this very thing, that he which hath begun a good work in you will perform it until the day of Jesus Christ." This verse reminds believers that God, who has started a work of restoration in their lives, will continue to be involved in that process until it is fully completed. However, this ongoing work requires periodic reflection, much like how a doctor regularly checks the progress of a healing bone. In the spiritual journey, these check-ups might involve personal reflection, prayer, reading scripture, or seeking counsel from a trusted spiritual mentor. These moments of reflection allow the individual to assess their spiritual growth, recognize areas where they might still be struggling, and seek God's guidance on how to continue moving forward. Just as a doctor monitors the physical healing of a bone, believers are called to regularly examine their hearts and lives to ensure they are growing in their faith and staying aligned with God's will. These spiritual check-ups are crucial because, without them, it's easy to become complacent or to overlook areas that still need healing or growth. For example, someone might initially experience a significant spiritual breakthrough, but over time, they might start to drift away from the practices and disciplines that helped them grow in the first place. Regular spiritual check-ups help to prevent this drift by keeping the individual focused and accountable. They provide a chance to recalibrate, to make sure that the work God has begun in their life is continuing to progress as it should. Just as in the physical realm, where a lack of check-ups can lead to complications or incomplete healing, a lack of spiritual check-ups can result in stagnation or even regression in one's faith journey. These check-ups are not just about identifying problems; they are also about celebrating progress and recognizing the ways in which God is working in one's life. Just as a doctor might show a patient how much their bone has healed since the last visit, these spiritual reflections can reveal how much growth and transformation have taken place over time. This can be incredibly encouraging and can provide the motivation needed to keep moving forward, even when the process is slow or challenging. Additionally, periodic check-ups in both contexts serve as a reminder that healing, whether physical or spiritual, is a process that takes time and requires patience. It's not something that happens overnight, but rather something that unfolds gradually, often with ups and downs along the way. By staying committed to these regular check-ins, the individual can stay on course, making adjustments as needed and ensuring that they are doing everything possible to support their healing and growth. This ongoing attention to the process is what ultimately leads to a full and complete recovery, whether it's a bone that is healing or a life that is being restored by God's grace. It's also worth noting that these check-ups provide an opportunity for the individual to receive encouragement and support from others, whether it's a doctor offering reassurance that the bone is healing well, or a spiritual mentor providing wisdom and guidance on the path of restoration. This external support can be invaluable, helping the person stay focused and committed to the healing process. In summary, periodic check-ups are a vital part of both physical healing and spiritual restoration. For a broken bone, these check-ups involve regular visits to the doctor to monitor the healing process, make any necessary adjustments, and ensure that the bone is mending correctly. For spiritual restoration, these check-ups involve regular moments of reflection, prayer, and seeking God's guidance to ensure that the individual is growing in their faith and staying on the path that God has set for them. In both cases, these check-ups are crucial for ensuring that the healing process is progressing as it should and for making any necessary adjustments to support full recovery. By staying committed to these regular check-ins, the individual can ensure that they are on the right track, whether they are healing from a physical injury or growing in their spiritual life. Ultimately, these periodic check-ups help to ensure that the work of healing, whether it's a broken bone or a broken spirit, is completed fully and effectively, leading to a life that is restored, whole, and strong.

Chapter 6 - Physical Therapy

Physical therapy is an essential step in the healing process after a bone has been broken and set because it helps restore strength, function, and mobility to the injured area, ensuring that the body can return to its normal activities without limitations or pain. When someone breaks a bone, the initial focus is on setting the bone back into its correct position and protecting it as it heals, usually with the help of a cast or splint. However, even after the bone has healed, the journey to full recovery is not yet complete. This is where physical therapy comes in. Once the cast or splint is removed, the muscles, tendons, and ligaments around the healed bone might be weak or stiff from lack of use during the immobilization period. The joint might also be less flexible, and the overall strength of the limb could be significantly reduced. Physical therapy is designed to address these issues by gradually reintroducing movement, strengthening the muscles, and improving the range of motion in the affected area. The process typically begins with gentle exercises to stretch and loosen the muscles and joints, which helps to improve flexibility and reduce stiffness. Over time, these exercises become more challenging as the body regains its strength and endurance. The physical therapist will guide the patient through various activities that target specific muscle groups and movements to ensure that the injured area is being worked on effectively without causing further harm. This might include weight-bearing exercises, resistance training, and activities that simulate everyday movements, such as walking, lifting, or bending. The goal is to restore full function to the affected area so that the patient can return to their normal routine without pain or limitations. Physical therapy is a gradual process, and it requires patience, commitment, and effort from the patient. It can be challenging and sometimes even uncomfortable, as the body is pushed to regain what it has lost during the immobilization period. However, this discomfort is a necessary part of the healing process because it signals that the body is rebuilding strength and flexibility. Without physical therapy, there is a risk that the injured area might not fully recover, leading to long-term issues such as chronic pain, reduced mobility, or a higher likelihood of re-injury. Therefore, physical therapy is crucial for ensuring a complete and successful recovery, allowing the patient to return to their normal life with confidence and strength. In the context of Christian restoration, the concept of physical therapy can be likened to the spiritual discipline and trials that believers undergo to strengthen their faith and character. Hebrews 12:11 says, "Now no chastening for the present seemeth to be joyous, but grievous: nevertheless afterward it yieldeth the peaceable fruit of righteousness unto them which are exercised thereby." This verse acknowledges that discipline, like physical therapy, is not always pleasant at the moment. It can be difficult, painful, and challenging, but it is ultimately beneficial for spiritual growth and maturity. Just as physical therapy is necessary to restore strength and function to a healed bone, spiritual discipline and trials are necessary to fortify a believer's faith and character. When a person goes through difficult times, whether it's personal struggles, challenges, or even failures, these experiences can be seen as spiritual "therapy" that helps them grow stronger in their faith. These trials test and refine their character, much like how physical therapy tests and strengthens the body. The discomfort and challenges faced during these times are not meaningless; they serve a purpose in helping the believer develop resilience, patience, and a deeper reliance on God. Over time, just as physical therapy leads to restored physical health, spiritual discipline and trials lead to a stronger, more mature faith. The "peaceable fruit of righteousness" mentioned in Hebrews is the result of enduring these challenges and coming out on the other side stronger and more grounded in one's faith. This process requires a similar level of commitment, patience, and effort as physical therapy. It's not easy, and it often requires pushing through difficult and uncomfortable situations, but the rewards are worth it. Just as a person who completes physical therapy is able to return to their normal life with strength and confidence, a believer who endures spiritual trials and discipline emerges with a stronger, more resilient faith that is better equipped to handle future challenges. In both physical and spiritual contexts, the process of therapy or discipline is essential for complete recovery and growth. It ensures that the individual is not just healed on the surface but is truly restored in a way that allows them to move forward with confidence and strength. The journey might be difficult, and there might be times when it feels overwhelming, but it is through these challenges that true growth occurs. The discomfort experienced during physical therapy is a sign that the body is healing and regaining its strength, just as the challenges faced during spiritual discipline are a sign that the believer is growing and maturing in their faith. Both processes are transformative, taking something that was broken and making it whole again, stronger than before. Physical therapy and spiritual discipline both require guidance, whether from a physical therapist or from God, to ensure that the process is carried out correctly and effectively. In physical therapy, the therapist designs a plan that is tailored to the patient's specific needs and abilities, guiding them through each step of the process to ensure they are making progress and not causing further harm. Similarly, in spiritual restoration, God provides guidance through His Word, through prayer, and through the counsel of others to help the believer navigate the challenges they face and grow in their faith. This guidance is crucial because it ensures that the process is carried out in a way that leads to true healing and growth, rather than just a superficial recovery. It is through this process of physical therapy or spiritual discipline that the individual is able to fully recover and become stronger, more resilient, and more capable of facing the challenges that life may bring. In conclusion, physical therapy is an essential part of the healing process for a broken bone, just as spiritual discipline and trials are essential for the restoration and growth of a believer's faith. Both processes involve challenges and discomfort, but they are necessary for achieving full recovery and strength. Physical therapy helps to restore strength, function, and mobility to the injured area, ensuring that the body can return to normal activities without pain or limitations. Similarly, spiritual discipline and trials help to strengthen a believer's faith and character, leading to spiritual maturity and the "peaceable fruit of righteousness" mentioned in Hebrews 12:11. Both processes require commitment, patience, and effort, but the rewards are worth it, leading to a stronger, more resilient individual who is better equipped to face future challenges with confidence and strength. Through physical therapy and spiritual discipline, what was once broken is made whole again, stronger and more capable than before.

Chapter 7 - Proper Nutrition

Proper nutrition plays a crucial role in both physical healing and spiritual restoration, serving as the foundation upon which recovery and growth are built. When someone breaks a bone, the body needs more than just medical intervention, such as setting the bone or applying a cast, to heal properly. Good nutrition is essential because it provides the body with the necessary building blocks to repair and strengthen the injured area. After a bone is broken, the body enters a state of increased metabolic activity as it works to mend the fracture. This process requires a variety of nutrients, including calcium, vitamin D, protein, and other vitamins and minerals that support bone health and tissue repair. Calcium is particularly important because it is the primary component of bone tissue. When a bone is healing, the body needs extra calcium to rebuild the bone matrix and ensure that the new bone tissue is strong and resilient. Vitamin D is also critical because it helps the body absorb calcium from the diet and supports the immune system, which plays a role in the healing process. Protein is another key nutrient, as it provides the amino acids necessary for repairing and rebuilding tissues, including bone, muscle, and skin. Other nutrients, such as vitamin C, magnesium, and zinc, also contribute to bone healing by supporting collagen formation, maintaining bone density, and promoting cellular repair. Without proper nutrition, the healing process can be delayed or incomplete, leading to weaker bones, prolonged recovery times, and an increased risk of complications. For example, a diet lacking in calcium and vitamin D might result in a bone that doesn't heal as strongly as it should, making it more susceptible to future fractures. Similarly, insufficient protein intake can slow down the repair of tissues surrounding the bone, leading to stiffness, weakness, and reduced mobility. Therefore, it's essential for individuals recovering from a bone injury to consume a well-balanced diet rich in these vital nutrients. This might include foods like dairy products, leafy green vegetables, fish, lean meats, nuts, seeds, and fortified cereals, all of which provide the nutrients needed to support bone healing and overall recovery. In addition to the specific nutrients required for bone healing, overall good nutrition is important for maintaining general health and well-being during the recovery process. When the body is well-nourished, it is better equipped to handle the demands of healing, including managing inflammation, repairing tissues, and fighting off infections. Proper hydration is also a key component of good nutrition, as it helps to transport nutrients to cells, remove waste products, and maintain the balance of fluids and electrolytes in the body. Just as physical healing from a bone injury requires proper nutrition, spiritual restoration also depends on receiving the right kind of nourishment, which, according to Matthew 4:4, comes from the Word of God. Jesus said, "Man shall not live by bread alone, but by every word that proceedeth out of the mouth of God." This verse emphasizes the importance of spiritual nourishment in sustaining and growing a believer's faith. Just as the body needs physical food to survive and thrive, the soul needs spiritual food to maintain its strength and vitality. The Word of God serves as this spiritual nourishment, providing the guidance, wisdom, and encouragement necessary for a Christian to grow in their faith and overcome the challenges they face. Without regular intake of God's Word, a believer's spiritual health can suffer, much like how the body would struggle without proper nutrition. A lack of spiritual nourishment can lead to a weakened faith, vulnerability to temptation, and a diminished ability to cope with life's difficulties. Just as poor nutrition can delay physical healing, neglecting spiritual nourishment can hinder a Christian's spiritual growth and restoration. Therefore, it is essential for believers to feed on God's Word regularly, allowing it to nourish their souls and strengthen their relationship with God. This spiritual nourishment comes from reading and meditating on the Bible, which is described as the "bread of life" that sustains believers and helps them grow in righteousness. The Bible offers more than just rules and teachings; it provides the spiritual sustenance that believers need to navigate life's challenges and continue growing in their faith. In the same way that a balanced diet provides the body with the necessary nutrients for physical healing, a balanced spiritual diet that includes regular Bible study, prayer, worship, and fellowship with other believers provides the soul with the sustenance it needs for spiritual restoration and growth. Just as physical nutrition supports the body's healing processes, spiritual nutrition through God's Word supports the soul's healing and growth, leading to a stronger, more resilient faith. Moreover, spiritual nourishment is not just about personal growth; it also equips believers to help others in their spiritual journeys. Just as good nutrition enables the body to function at its best, spiritual nourishment empowers believers to serve others, share their faith, and live out the principles of the Bible in their daily lives. In this way, spiritual nourishment has a ripple effect, impacting not only the individual believer but also those around them. It's important to recognize that both physical and spiritual nutrition require consistency. Just as one healthy meal won't sustain the body for long, one reading of the Bible or one prayer session won't sustain the soul indefinitely. Regular, consistent intake of both physical and spiritual nourishment is necessary to maintain health and strength over time. This means making good nutrition and spiritual practices a part of one's daily routine, ensuring that both the body and the soul receive the sustenance they need to thrive. Proper nutrition, whether physical or spiritual, is foundational to the healing and growth process. It's about providing the body and the soul with the necessary tools to repair, rebuild, and strengthen themselves. Just as a well-nourished body is better equipped to heal from a bone injury, a well-nourished soul is better equipped to grow in faith and overcome the challenges of life. This nourishment is not just about survival; it's about thriving and reaching one's full potential, whether physically or spiritually. In conclusion, proper nutrition is a critical component of both physical healing and spiritual restoration. For someone recovering from a broken bone, good nutrition provides the essential nutrients needed to repair and strengthen the bone, ensuring a complete and successful recovery. For a believer seeking spiritual restoration, regular nourishment from God's Word is essential for sustaining and growing their faith. Both forms of nourishment are vital for achieving health and strength, enabling individuals to live full, active, and purposeful lives. Just as the body cannot thrive without the right nutrients, the soul cannot thrive without the spiritual sustenance provided by God's Word. Therefore, it is important to prioritize proper nutrition in all aspects of life, recognizing that it is the foundation upon which healing, growth, and overall well-being are built. Whether it's through a balanced diet or regular engagement with the Bible, proper nourishment is the key to achieving and maintaining health, strength, and vitality, both physically and spiritually.

Chapter 8 - Prevention of Re-injury

Prevention of re-injury is a crucial aspect of both physical recovery and spiritual restoration, as it ensures that the healing process is not undone and that the individual can continue to live a healthy, fulfilling life without the fear of falling back into old patterns of harm or injury. When someone suffers from a broken bone, the initial stages of treatment focus on setting the bone correctly and providing the necessary conditions for it to heal, such as immobilization through a cast or splint. However, once the bone has healed, the journey is not over. One of the most important aspects of recovery is taking measures to prevent re-injury. This involves a combination of physical therapy, lifestyle adjustments, and awareness to ensure that the bone remains strong and does not suffer further damage. For instance, after the removal of a cast, the muscles around the healed bone are often weak due to the lack of use, and the joint might be stiff. Physical therapy helps to restore strength and flexibility, but it also teaches the individual how to move and use the affected area safely to avoid putting unnecessary strain on it. This might include exercises to improve balance and coordination, learning proper techniques for lifting or bending, and gradually increasing the intensity of physical activities to avoid overloading the healing bone. Additionally, individuals are often advised to make certain lifestyle changes, such as avoiding high-impact sports or activities that pose a risk of falling or direct impact on the injured area, at least until full strength and stability are regained. This might also involve wearing protective gear, like braces or pads, during physical activities to provide extra support and reduce the risk of re-injury. In some cases, individuals might need to adjust their daily routines or find alternative ways to perform tasks that previously put them at risk of injury. For example, someone who has broken a leg might need to be more cautious when walking on uneven surfaces or climbing stairs, while someone who has injured their wrist might need to modify their approach to tasks that involve repetitive motions, like typing or lifting. The key is to be mindful of the factors that led to the initial injury and to take proactive steps to avoid those situations in the future. Prevention of re-injury is not just about physical precautions; it's also about mental and emotional awareness. Fear of re-injury can sometimes be a significant barrier to recovery, causing individuals to hold back or avoid activities they previously enjoyed out of concern that they might get hurt again. While it's important to be cautious, it's also crucial to rebuild confidence and trust in one's body. This might involve gradually reintroducing activities, starting with low-risk exercises and slowly progressing to more challenging ones as confidence and strength build. Working with a physical therapist or trainer can provide guidance and support during this phase, helping individuals to push past their fears while still taking appropriate precautions. Just as prevention of re-injury is critical in physical recovery, it is equally important in the context of Christian restoration. The Bible, in Ephesians 6:11, instructs believers to "Put on the whole armour of God, that ye may be able to stand against the wiles of the devil." This verse highlights the need for spiritual protection to prevent falling back into sin or harmful behaviors after a period of restoration. Just as a healed bone can be vulnerable to re-injury if not properly protected, a restored Christian can be vulnerable to spiritual harm if they do not take steps to guard themselves against temptation and the challenges of the world. The "armor of God" described in Ephesians 6 includes elements such as the belt of truth, the breastplate of righteousness, the shield of faith, the helmet of salvation, and the sword of the Spirit, which is the word of God. Each piece of this spiritual armor serves a specific purpose in protecting the believer from the various "wiles of the devil," which can include temptation, doubt, fear, and other forms of spiritual attack. Just as physical armor protects a soldier in battle, the armor of God provides the spiritual protection needed to stand firm in faith and avoid falling back into old patterns of sin or despair. Wearing this armor involves being constantly vigilant and aware of the spiritual dangers that can lead to re-injury. This might include regular prayer, Bible study, and fellowship with other believers to stay grounded in faith and connected to God's guidance. It also involves making conscious choices to avoid situations, people, or environments that might lead to temptation or spiritual compromise. For example, someone who has struggled with addiction might need to avoid certain social settings or relationships that could trigger a relapse, while someone who has struggled with anger might need to practice mindfulness and self-control in stressful situations to avoid falling back into harmful patterns. Just as in physical recovery, the goal is to be proactive in preventing re-injury rather than reactive. This means identifying potential risks and taking steps to mitigate them before they become a problem. It also means staying humble and recognizing that even after restoration, the risk of falling back into old habits or sins remains if one is not careful. Regular self-reflection and accountability can help in this regard, providing a way to check in with oneself and others to ensure that the steps being taken are effective and that the armor is being worn properly. Moreover, prevention of re-injury in a spiritual sense also involves nurturing the new growth and strength that have come from the restoration process. Just as a healed bone might be stronger in some ways due to the healing process, a restored Christian can emerge from their struggles with a deeper faith, greater resilience, and a stronger relationship with God. However, this new strength needs to be maintained and cultivated through ongoing spiritual discipline, much like how physical strength needs to be maintained through regular exercise and proper care. This might involve continuing the practices that helped in the initial restoration, such as daily prayer, regular church attendance, or involvement in a small group or Bible study. It might also involve seeking out new opportunities for growth, such as serving others, sharing one's testimony, or taking on new challenges in faith. The key is to keep moving forward, building on the progress that has been made, and not becoming complacent or overconfident. In both physical and spiritual contexts, the prevention of re-injury is about protecting the progress that has been made and ensuring that the healing process is not undone. It's about being mindful of the risks and taking proactive steps to mitigate them, whether that involves wearing protective gear, practicing safe movements, or staying grounded in faith and connected to God's guidance. It's also about building confidence and trust in the new strength and resilience that have come from the healing process, while still recognizing the need for ongoing care and vigilance. In summary, prevention of re-injury is an essential part of both physical recovery and spiritual restoration. For someone who has healed from a broken bone, this involves taking measures to protect the injury from further harm, such as through physical therapy, lifestyle adjustments, and mental awareness. For a believer who has been restored spiritually, this involves wearing the armor of God and taking steps to protect oneself from spiritual harm, such as through regular prayer, Bible study, and conscious choices to avoid temptation. In both cases, the goal is to protect the progress that has been made and to continue moving forward with confidence and strength, while still being mindful of the risks and taking appropriate precautions. By doing so, individuals can ensure that their recovery, whether physical or spiritual, is complete and lasting, allowing them to live a healthy, fulfilling life without fear of falling back into old patterns of harm or injury.

Chapter 9 - Patience in Healing

Patience in healing is an essential aspect of both physical recovery and spiritual restoration, serving as a vital reminder that true healing, whether of the body or the spirit, requires time, perseverance, and trust in the process. When someone suffers from a broken bone, the journey to full recovery is not immediate; it's a gradual process that demands patience and care. After the bone has been set and the initial treatment has been administered, the body needs time to heal the injury. This process involves the body's natural ability to regenerate and repair the damaged bone tissue, which happens in stages and cannot be rushed. The first stage of healing typically involves inflammation, where the body sends blood to the injured area to start the repair process. This is followed by the production of a soft callus, which is a type of tissue that begins to bridge the gap between the broken bone ends. Over time, this soft callus is replaced by a hard callus, which eventually turns into new bone. Finally, the bone is remodeled to return to its original shape and strength. Each of these stages takes time, and while it might be tempting to wish for a quick recovery, patience is crucial. Rushing the process or not allowing enough time for proper healing can lead to complications, such as the bone not healing correctly, which might result in a weaker bone, prolonged pain, or the need for further medical intervention. For example, if someone tries to resume their normal activities too soon after a bone injury, they might risk re-injury or cause the bone to heal improperly, leading to long-term issues. This is why doctors often emphasize the importance of following their recommendations, such as wearing a cast or splint for the prescribed amount of time, avoiding certain activities, and attending follow-up appointments to monitor the healing progress. Patience during this time is not just about waiting passively; it's an active process of taking care of oneself, following medical advice, and trusting that the body will heal in its own time. In many ways, this patience is a form of discipline, as it requires resisting the urge to do too much too soon and instead focusing on what's best for the long-term health and recovery of the injured area. Just as patience is essential in the physical healing process, it is equally important in the context of Christian restoration. The Bible, in Isaiah 40:31, says, "But they that wait upon the LORD shall renew their strength; they shall mount up with wings as eagles; they shall run, and not be weary; and they shall walk, and not faint." This verse speaks to the importance of waiting on God and trusting in His timing for full restoration. Just as a broken bone requires time to heal, so does the spirit, especially after it has been wounded by sin, loss, or other spiritual struggles. Spiritual healing is often a journey that involves periods of reflection, prayer, and growth. It's not something that can be hurried or forced, as true restoration comes from allowing God to work in His time and in His way. This process of waiting on the Lord is not always easy, as it can be difficult to remain patient when faced with the desire for immediate relief or resolution. However, just as with physical healing, rushing the process of spiritual restoration can lead to incomplete healing or even setbacks. For example, if someone tries to move on too quickly after a spiritual setback without fully addressing the underlying issues, they might find themselves struggling with the same problems again later on. Patience in this context means trusting that God knows the best path for healing and that He will bring about full restoration in His time. It also means being willing to go through the necessary steps of growth and learning, even when they are challenging or uncomfortable. This might involve facing difficult truths about oneself, making changes in one's life, or simply waiting for clarity and direction from God. The process of spiritual healing, much like physical healing, often involves stages of growth and transformation. There might be times when it feels like progress is slow or even non-existent, but it's important to remember that healing is happening, even if it's not immediately visible. Just as the body works quietly and steadily to heal a broken bone, God works in the heart and soul to bring about spiritual restoration, often in ways that we cannot see or fully understand in the moment. Patience during this time is a form of faith, as it requires trusting in God's plan and believing that He will bring about the best outcome, even when the path is unclear or the waiting is difficult. It's about letting go of the need for control and surrendering to God's timing and wisdom. In both physical and spiritual contexts, patience is not just about waiting; it's about actively participating in the healing process by doing what's necessary to support recovery. This might involve taking care of one's body by eating well, getting enough rest, and following medical advice, or it might involve nurturing one's spirit through prayer, Bible study, and seeking support from others. In both cases, patience is about allowing the process to unfold naturally and trusting that, in time, healing will come. It's also important to recognize that patience in healing involves dealing with setbacks and challenges along the way. There might be times when progress seems slow, or when it feels like things are moving backward instead of forward. In these moments, patience is about persevering, staying committed to the process, and not giving up, even when it's difficult. Just as a bone might ache or feel weak as it heals, the spirit might go through periods of doubt, fear, or frustration during the process of restoration. However, by remaining patient and trusting in the process, the individual can move through these challenges and come out stronger on the other side. In both physical and spiritual healing, patience ultimately leads to renewed strength and resilience. Just as a fully healed bone can be stronger than it was before the injury, a spirit that has been restored through patience and trust in God can emerge with greater faith, wisdom, and understanding. The process of healing, though slow and sometimes difficult, results in a deeper sense of wholeness and well-being that can only come from allowing the necessary time for recovery. In conclusion, patience in healing is a vital aspect of both physical recovery and spiritual restoration. For someone recovering from a broken bone, patience involves allowing the body the time it needs to heal properly, following medical advice, and resisting the urge to rush the process. For a believer seeking spiritual restoration, patience means waiting on God, trusting in His timing, and allowing the process of growth and healing to unfold naturally. In both cases, patience is key to achieving full restoration, as it allows for the necessary time and space for healing to occur. By embracing patience and trusting in the process, individuals can experience true healing and emerge stronger, more resilient, and more prepared to face the future with confidence and hope. Whether in the physical or spiritual realm, patience in healing is a discipline that ultimately leads to renewed strength and a deeper sense of wholeness, allowing for a full and lasting recovery that brings about true restoration and growth.

Chapter 10 - Permanent Mark (Scarring)

The concept of a permanent mark or scarring is deeply intertwined with the processes of both physical healing and spiritual restoration, representing not just the end of a painful experience but also the enduring memory and lessons that come from it. When someone suffers a physical injury, such as a broken bone, the body undergoes a remarkable process of healing, gradually repairing the damage and restoring functionality. However, even after the bone has mended, the body often bears a scar—a permanent mark that remains as a testament to the injury that once was. Scarring is a natural part of the healing process, resulting from the body's effort to close and repair the wound. When the skin or tissue is damaged, the body produces collagen, a protein that helps to knit the tissue back together. This new tissue, while functional, is not exactly the same as the original tissue; it is often tougher, less flexible, and has a different texture or color. The scar that forms is a visible reminder of the trauma that occurred, and while it may fade over time, it never completely disappears. In some cases, scars can be quite noticeable, while in others they may be faint and only visible under certain conditions. Regardless of their appearance, scars are a testament to the body's ability to heal itself, a symbol of survival and resilience. They remind the individual of the pain and difficulty they endured, but they also serve as proof that they overcame it. In this way, scars are both a physical and emotional marker of the experience, carrying with them the story of what happened and the strength that was gained in the process. Just as physical scars are a natural outcome of healing, spiritual scars are often the result of the restoration process in a believer's life. The Bible, in Galatians 6:17, speaks of bearing the "marks of the Lord Jesus," which can be understood as the spiritual scars or permanent marks left by the trials and challenges faced in the journey of faith. These marks, like physical scars, are not something to be ashamed of; rather, they are a powerful testimony to the struggles endured and the victories won. In the spiritual context, scars represent the growth and transformation that occur through difficult experiences. Just as a physical scar may remind someone of a past injury or surgery, a spiritual scar might remind a believer of a time when their faith was tested, when they faced significant challenges, or when they had to rely on God's strength to get through a difficult season. These experiences, while painful, often lead to greater spiritual maturity and a deeper understanding of one's relationship with God. The scars left behind serve as reminders of God's faithfulness, of the lessons learned, and of the strength that was developed in the process. They are not just symbols of past pain but also of the healing and restoration that followed. Spiritual scars can take many forms—they might be the lingering effects of a past sin that has been forgiven but not forgotten, the memory of a difficult decision made in faith, or the awareness of a weakness that was once a source of shame but has now become a source of strength. These marks are part of the believer's story, woven into the fabric of their spiritual journey. They serve as reminders of where they have been, how far they have come, and how God has worked in their lives to bring them through their trials. In this way, spiritual scars are not a sign of weakness but of resilience and growth. They show that the believer has faced adversity and come out stronger on the other side. Just as a healed bone is often stronger at the site of the break, a believer's faith can become stronger after going through a period of testing and restoration. The scars left behind are evidence of this growth, a visible sign of the internal transformation that has taken place. These marks also serve as a source of encouragement and inspiration, both to the individual who bears them and to others who might be going through similar struggles. Seeing someone who has survived a difficult experience and come out stronger can give hope to those who are still in the midst of their own challenges. It can be a powerful reminder that healing and restoration are possible, even if the process leaves behind scars. In both physical and spiritual healing, scars are a natural and expected outcome. They are a part of the healing process, a sign that the body or soul has done its work to repair the damage and move forward. While scars might not be aesthetically pleasing, they carry deep meaning and significance. They are a testament to survival, resilience, and the ability to overcome adversity. In some cases, scars might cause discomfort or self-consciousness, especially if they are in a visible or prominent location. However, with time, many people come to accept and even embrace their scars as part of their personal story. They might see them as a badge of honor, a reminder of what they have been through and how they have grown. In the same way, spiritual scars might be a source of pain or discomfort at first, especially if they are the result of deep wounds or significant challenges. But over time, as healing takes place, these scars can become a source of strength and a reminder of God's grace and faithfulness. They can serve as a powerful testimony to others, showing that even in the midst of trials, there is hope and the possibility of restoration. The idea of bearing scars, whether physical or spiritual, is a reminder that healing is not always about returning to the way things were before. Instead, it's about moving forward with the knowledge and strength gained from the experience. Scars are a part of that journey, a permanent mark that tells the story of what happened and how it changed the individual. They are a visible sign of the invisible work that has taken place within the body or soul, a reminder that while the past cannot be erased, it can be redeemed and transformed into something that brings strength and resilience. In conclusion, the concept of a permanent mark or scarring is a powerful symbol in both physical and spiritual healing. In the physical sense, a scar is a natural outcome of the body's healing process, a reminder of the injury that was endured and the strength that was gained in overcoming it. In the spiritual sense, scars represent the growth and transformation that occur through trials and challenges, a visible sign of the internal work that has taken place. While scars might not be something that people seek out, they are an inevitable part of the healing journey, a reminder of the pain that was endured and the strength that was gained. They serve as a testimony to survival, resilience, and the ability to overcome adversity, both in the body and in the spirit. Whether physical or spiritual, scars are a part of the story of healing, a permanent mark that reminds us of where we have been, how far we have come, and the strength that has been developed along the way. They are a symbol of the journey, a visible sign of the invisible work that has taken place, and a reminder that while the past may leave its mark, it can also lead to growth, strength, and transformation.

Chapter 11 - Performance Restoration

Performance restoration is a critical and final stage in the journey of both physical healing and spiritual restoration, aiming to bring an individual back to full use, functionality, and purpose in their life. When someone suffers a physical injury, such as a broken bone, the initial focus is on diagnosing the injury, setting the bone correctly, and ensuring proper healing through immobilization, pain management, and protection. However, the ultimate goal of this entire process is to restore the person's ability to use the affected limb or body part as they did before the injury occurred, if not better. This phase is what is known as performance restoration, and it is crucial because it determines whether the individual can return to their normal activities, including work, hobbies, and daily tasks, without limitations, pain, or fear of re-injury. Performance restoration is not just about the bone healing or the injury mending; it's about regaining full strength, flexibility, coordination, and confidence in the use of the body part that was injured. This process often involves physical therapy, where the patient is guided through a series of exercises and activities designed to rebuild muscle strength, enhance joint flexibility, and improve overall coordination and balance. Physical therapy is tailored to the specific needs of the patient and the nature of the injury, gradually increasing in intensity and complexity as the patient regains their abilities. The goal is to ensure that by the end of the therapy, the patient is not only free from pain and discomfort but also fully capable of performing all the tasks they could before the injury, if not with greater proficiency. For example, if someone broke their leg, performance restoration would involve regaining the ability to walk, run, jump, and perform other activities without hesitation or difficulty. This process might take weeks or even months, depending on the severity of the injury and the patient's dedication to their recovery program. The key to successful performance restoration is persistence and patience, as it requires the individual to push through challenges, setbacks, and the natural frustrations that come with rebuilding physical capabilities. The same concept of performance restoration applies to spiritual restoration in the context of Christian faith. When someone goes through a period of spiritual struggle, whether due to sin, loss, doubt, or other challenges, the journey to restoration is not complete until they have fully regained their spiritual strength, purpose, and functionality in their faith. Psalm 23:3 states, "He restoreth my soul: he leadeth me in the paths of righteousness for his name's sake." This verse speaks to the process of spiritual performance restoration, where God not only heals the soul from its wounds but also leads the believer back to a life of righteousness and purpose. Just as physical therapy is necessary to restore physical performance, spiritual practices and disciplines are essential to restore spiritual performance. This might include regular prayer, Bible study, worship, and fellowship with other believers, all of which help to rebuild the individual's spiritual strength and guide them back to a path of righteousness. The goal of spiritual performance restoration is not just to return the believer to their previous state of faith but to bring them to a place of even greater spiritual maturity, purpose, and alignment with God's will. This process, like physical performance restoration, requires time, effort, and dedication. It often involves facing and overcoming spiritual challenges, such as dealing with lingering doubts, overcoming temptations, and rebuilding a relationship with God that may have been strained or weakened. Through this process, the believer is gradually restored to full spiritual functionality, able to live out their faith with confidence, strength, and purpose. They become more resilient in their faith, better equipped to handle future challenges, and more deeply rooted in their relationship with God. Performance restoration in both physical and spiritual contexts is about achieving a state of wholeness and functionality that allows the individual to live fully and purposefully. In the case of a broken bone, this means being able to use the limb or body part as effectively as before the injury, without pain or limitations. In the case of spiritual restoration, it means living a life that is fully aligned with God's will, guided by righteousness, and filled with a sense of purpose and direction. This restored state is not just about recovery; it's about thriving and fulfilling one's potential in every aspect of life. In both scenarios, performance restoration is a journey that requires persistence, commitment, and trust in the process. It's about pushing through the difficult moments, staying focused on the goal, and allowing the necessary time for full recovery and growth. Just as a patient in physical therapy must be diligent in their exercises and follow their therapist's guidance, a believer in spiritual restoration must be diligent in their spiritual practices and follow God's guidance. The rewards of this process are profound, leading to a life that is not only healed but also enriched, empowered, and ready to take on new challenges with renewed strength and confidence. In conclusion, performance restoration is the final and perhaps most important phase of both physical healing and spiritual restoration. It's about regaining full functionality, strength, and purpose in the area that was injured or weakened, whether that's a physical limb or a spiritual aspect of life. This process involves dedication, hard work, and the willingness to push through challenges, but it ultimately leads to a state of wholeness and readiness to engage fully in life's activities, whether they be physical tasks or spiritual missions. By embracing the process of performance restoration, individuals can achieve a level of recovery and growth that not only restores them to their former capabilities but also prepares them for even greater achievements and deeper fulfillment in the future. Whether it's the ability to walk without pain after a broken leg or the ability to live out one's faith with renewed vigor after a period of spiritual struggle, performance restoration is about reclaiming one's life and moving forward with confidence, strength, and a clear sense of purpose.

Chapter 12 - Persistent Care

'Persistent care is an essential component of both physical recovery and spiritual restoration, as it ensures that the healing and growth achieved during the initial stages are maintained over the long term. When someone suffers a physical injury, such as a broken bone, the process of healing doesn't end once the bone has mended. In fact, what happens after the bone has healed is just as important as the initial treatment, because ongoing care is necessary to ensure that the injury doesn't lead to future problems and that the affected area remains healthy and functional. This concept of persistent care involves a combination of activities and practices that are designed to support the body's continued recovery and prevent any recurrence of the injury. For instance, after a bone has been set and has healed, it's crucial to continue with physical therapy to rebuild strength, flexibility, and coordination in the muscles and joints around the healed bone. This helps to restore full functionality and reduces the risk of re-injury. The patient might also be advised to maintain a healthy diet rich in nutrients that support bone health, such as calcium and vitamin D, and to engage in regular exercise that promotes overall physical fitness and well-being. Additionally, ongoing medical check-ups might be necessary to monitor the healed bone and ensure that there are no complications, such as bone density loss or improper healing, that could cause problems in the future. Persistent care is about being proactive in maintaining the health and functionality of the body, recognizing that the work of healing is not complete once the immediate injury has been addressed, but rather, it continues as the body adapts and strengthens over time. This same principle of persistent care applies to spiritual restoration, where the goal is not just to restore a believer's relationship with God after a period of struggle, but to maintain and nurture that relationship on an ongoing basis. In John 15:4, Jesus says, "Abide in me, and I in you. As the branch cannot bear fruit of itself, except it abide in the vine; no more can ye, except ye abide in me." This verse underscores the importance of continuous spiritual care, emphasizing that a believer's connection to Christ must be maintained in order to sustain spiritual health and growth. Just as a branch cannot thrive or produce fruit if it is disconnected from the vine, a believer cannot maintain a strong, vibrant spiritual life without ongoing care and a close, abiding relationship with Christ. Persistent spiritual care involves regular practices that keep a believer connected to God and growing in their faith. This includes daily prayer, which allows the believer to communicate with God, express their thoughts and feelings, and seek guidance and strength for the challenges they face. It also includes regular reading and meditation on the Bible, which serves as spiritual nourishment, providing wisdom, encouragement, and insight into God's will. Worship and fellowship with other believers are also important components of persistent spiritual care, as they provide opportunities for communal support, shared faith experiences, and mutual encouragement. Just as the body needs regular exercise and proper nutrition to stay healthy, the spirit needs regular spiritual practices to stay strong and vibrant. Without this ongoing care, a believer's spiritual life can become stagnant, leading to a weakening of their faith and a greater susceptibility to temptation, doubt, and other spiritual challenges. Persistent care in the spiritual sense is about more than just maintaining the status quo; it's about continually growing and deepening one's relationship with God. This might involve setting aside time each day to reflect on God's presence in one's life, to give thanks for blessings received, and to seek guidance for the future. It might also involve engaging in acts of service, which allow the believer to live out their faith in practical ways and to experience the joy and fulfillment that comes from helping others. Just as persistent care in the physical sense involves taking proactive steps to maintain health and prevent re-injury, persistent spiritual care involves taking proactive steps to nurture one's relationship with God and to prevent spiritual backsliding. This might include regularly examining one's heart and life to identify areas where growth is needed, and then taking steps to address those areas through prayer, study, and intentional changes in behavior. It might also involve seeking out new opportunities for spiritual growth, such as joining a Bible study group, attending a retreat, or exploring new ways to serve in the church or community. The goal of persistent care, whether physical or spiritual, is to ensure that the progress made during the initial stages of healing is not lost, but rather, is built upon and expanded. In both contexts, persistent care requires commitment, discipline, and a long-term perspective. It's about recognizing that healing and growth are ongoing processes, not one-time events, and that maintaining health—whether of the body or the spirit—requires regular attention and effort. This ongoing care helps to prevent setbacks and ensures that the individual can continue to live a full, healthy, and purposeful life. In the physical realm, persistent care might mean continuing with exercises and healthy habits long after the bone has healed, to ensure that the body remains strong and resilient. In the spiritual realm, it means continuing to seek God, to abide in Him, and to grow in faith, long after the initial period of restoration has passed. This approach to care is not about being fearful or overly cautious, but about being wise and intentional in how one lives, recognizing that the choices made each day contribute to long-term health and well-being. Persistent care is also about being adaptable and responsive to changing needs and circumstances. Just as a person's physical health might require different types of care at different stages of life, so too might their spiritual needs evolve over time. Persistent spiritual care involves being attuned to these changes and being willing to adjust one's practices and priorities accordingly. This might mean deepening one's prayer life during times of crisis, seeking out new forms of spiritual nourishment when old ones no longer seem effective, or finding new ways to connect with God and others as life circumstances change. Ultimately, persistent care is about fostering a lifestyle that supports ongoing health, growth, and fulfillment, in both the physical and spiritual dimensions of life. It's about making choices that align with long-term goals and values, and about being consistent in the practices that support those goals. Whether it's the daily habits that keep the body strong or the spiritual disciplines that keep the soul connected to God, persistent care is the key to maintaining the progress made during the initial stages of healing and ensuring that it lasts for a lifetime. In conclusion, persistent care is an essential aspect of both physical recovery and spiritual restoration, ensuring that the gains made during the initial healing process are maintained and built upon over time. In the context of physical healing, this involves ongoing practices such as physical therapy, proper nutrition, regular exercise, and medical check-ups, all of which help to keep the body strong, functional, and resilient. In the context of spiritual restoration, persistent care involves abiding in Christ, engaging in regular prayer, Bible study, worship, and fellowship, and continually seeking to grow and deepen one's relationship with God. Both forms of care require commitment, discipline, and a long-term perspective, recognizing that true healing and growth are ongoing processes that require regular attention and effort. By embracing the principles of persistent care, individuals can ensure that the progress made during the initial stages of healing is not only maintained but also expanded, leading to a life that is healthy, vibrant, and full of purpose, both physically and spiritually. Persistent care is the key to living a life that is not just about survival but about thriving, growing, and fulfilling one's potential in every area of life. Whether caring for the body or the spirit, persistent care is the foundation upon which long-term health and well-being are built, allowing individuals to live fully and purposefully, in alignment with their values and with God's will for their lives.

Conclusion

As we bring "Restoration: Setting the Bone" to a close, it is important to reflect on the profound journey of healing and renewal that God invites every Christian to undertake. The metaphor of setting a bone is not just an illustration but a powerful reminder that true restoration is a deliberate, careful process—one that requires both the skillful touch of the Great Physician and the patient cooperation of the believer. Just as a bone must be properly set to heal correctly, so too must our spiritual lives be realigned with God's will to experience true restoration and wholeness.

Throughout this book, we have explored the biblical principles of restoration, recognizing that the desire to be restored is a divine prompting—a call from God to return to Him and allow Him to mend what is broken. Whether the fractures in our lives stem from sin, emotional wounds, or the weariness of life's trials, the process of restoration is always available to us through the grace of Jesus Christ. The Bible is filled with stories of God's restorative work, demonstrating that no one is beyond His reach and that no situation is too hopeless for His healing power.

However, the journey of restoration doesn't end with healing; it continues with a commitment to maintain that restoration and to grow stronger in our faith. Just as a bone that has been set requires time to heal and regain strength, so too must we continue to nurture our restored spiritual lives. This involves ongoing discipline in prayer, Scripture study, fellowship with other believers, and a continual reliance on God's grace to sustain us. The restored life is not a return to what was, but a stepping into something new and even stronger—a life more deeply rooted in Christ and more fully aligned with His purposes.

As you move forward from this point, remember that restoration is both a one-time event and a continuous process. It begins with a decision to seek God's healing, but it requires daily choices to live in the reality of that restored relationship with Him. There will be challenges along the way—moments of doubt, temptations to return to old ways, and pressures from the world—but it is in these moments that you must cling to the truths you have learned. God's promises are steadfast, and His commitment to your restoration is unwavering.

"Restoration: Setting the Bone" is not just a guide for healing past wounds; it is a roadmap for living a restored life in the present and future. It is about embracing the new identity that God has given you in Christ and walking in the fullness of His grace every day. As you continue on your journey, let the lessons of this book serve as reminders of God's faithfulness, His desire for your wholeness, and His power to transform even the most broken areas of your life.

In conclusion, may you always remember that God's restoration is not simply about fixing what is broken, but about making all things new. As you continue to walk in His ways, trust that He will guide you, strengthen you, and lead you into the abundant life He has prepared for you. The bone has been set—now continue to grow strong in the Lord.

Don't miss out!

Visit the website below and you can sign up to receive emails whenever Joshua Rhoades publishes a new book. There's no charge and no obligation.

https://books2read.com/r/B-A-AJLBB-IMBYE

BOOKS2READ

Connecting independent readers to independent writers.

Did you love *Restoration - Setting The Bone*? Then you should read *Courage Under Fire: David's Stand On The Battlefield*[1] by Joshua Rhoades!

Courage Under Fire: David's Stand on the Battlefield" recounts the stirring first-person narrative of David, a young shepherd boy who faced the colossal Philistine warrior, Goliath, armed with nothing but a sling, a few stones, and an unwavering faith in God. My journey begins with my humble obedience to my father, Jesse, who sent me to deliver provisions to my brothers on the front lines. Despite their scoffing bond jeers at my presence on the battlefield, I remained undeterred, feeling a deep sense

1. https://books2read.com/u/3G7wPP

2. https://books2read.com/u/3G7wPP